WOUNDED BUD

SAINT JULIAN PRESS

"This book is a tavern. Enter it from any direction and drink. Each cup is a treasure, hand-crafted, unique, yet all contain the wine of astonishment and one full jigger of God's freshest glory. O, so delicious! I drank too many and reeled off my barstool into the evening. There I saw Whitman sail past the moon, old Khayyam was singing, and the Girl whom I'm planning on marrying whispered: Lo, these pages express what can never be seen, in words that describe what can never be said." ~Peter Hayes, Author of *The Supreme Adventure* and *My Lady of the Bog: An Archeo-Forensic Mystery*

"Fred LaMotte's poems come from the depth of silence. They are nourishment for the starving spirit, and spring water for the thirsty. They encourage the reader to leave worry and fear behind and return to the origin, the root of all roots. This is the kind of reminder we need in this troubled world that has forgotten how to smile." ~Guthema Roba, poet and author of *Please Come Home*

"A modern Rumi? Fred's poetry is rich with love, sensual and timeless, an exploration of what comes out of the stillness and silence of awakening. I have not read a book of contemporary poetry this wise and delightful in decades. As I do with the poetry of the masters, I will return to Fred's poetry again and again. It's a bit like reading Kabir for the first time but in your own language, and your own time. You read it and you know: this is a man who understands poetry, who understands spirit, who understands you." ~George Kinder, Buddhist meditation teacher, author of *Transforming Suffering into Wisdom*

"Discovering Fred LaMotte's poetry has been a true gift to me. His poems are beautifully-written portals to a high consciousness and, like all great poetry, expand the reader." ~Donna Baier Stein, Author of *Sympathetic People* and publisher of *Tiferet Journal*

"Fred's poetry speaks to my soul of long lost love and redeems my heart from a fall that I cannot even remember. Somehow he makes it all seem all right." ~Susanne Marie, Founder of Transformation through Presence

"Fred LaMotte's poems are passionate and rich, yet unusually spare, sewn together with fine mystical thread into beautiful creatures that breathe and live inside us long after we have met them. Reading his poetry is like drowning in nectar and seeing through liquid gold: we are immersed in the sweet taste of Truth." ~Aile Shebar, founder of Writing from the Heart™, and One Heart Productions, presenting audio-visual performances of poetry, mystical literature, and Sufi-inspired dance.

"Fred LaMotte's poetry is a living bridge between the boundless infinite and its expression: timeless vibration in words. Like a Rumi or Hafez, Fred has the rare and illumined skill of using words to unlock an inner door to the Innate Divine Presence. His poems are not just language, but vibrational medicine that help us remember home. His humor, sincerity, depth, compassion, and challenge are threads that weave a tapestry of transformational writing. We don't read the words of Fred LaMotte, we breathe them in as prayer, and let them melt our hearts open." ~Dr. Matt Lyon, Founder of Network Wellness Center and author of *Radical Healing*.

WOUNDED BUD

Poems

by

Alfred K. LaMotte

SAINT JULIAN PRESS

HOUSTON

Published by Saint Julian Press, Inc.

2053 Cortlandt, Suite 200

Houston, Texas 77008

www.saintjulianpress.com

ISBN-13: 978-0-9965231-6-5

ISBN: 0-9965231-6-2

Library of Congress Control Number: 2016932179

Cover photograph is a dahlia from the Pea Patch Community Garden in Seattle, Washington, courtesy of Abigail Fell LaMotte.

To my teacher, Shri Shri Guru Dev,
my wife Anna and my daughters Abby and Liz,
Dana the Muse, and the Goddess in all her forms.

TABLE OF CONTENTS

"Lovers find secret places inside this violent world, where they make transactions with beauty." ~Rumi

"The political problems of the world are the problems of the human heart. A love song can be the greatest act of protest." ~Bono

PREFACE

Silence is the mother. As the Word of creation is born from silence, so words of poetry, like prayer, can guide us back to creation's silent source. These poems invite you with joy, wonder, and sometimes humor, to a space of silence, the silence of meditation, the blue sky of prayer.

The early Christian Gnostic Valentinus said that the real Virgin Mother is "mystical eternal silence." Let us dance in the space between our thoughts, where love turns particles into waves. Poetry helps.

This book is for the table beside your meditation cushion, or your bedside, or the carry-on bag on you travels. But it's not for a bookshelf. I hope it gets dog-eared and frayed, used like a hand tool.

As an interfaith chaplain, I hope that your community might use these poems for discussion and empowerment in meditation circles. The first section contains seeds of meditation: "A Silence Between Thoughts."

As a citizen of the Earth, I embrace all wisdom paths as my heritage, and I honor all the world's scriptures as my birth-right. With deepest gratitude, I harvest these seeds from the fruits of several traditions: the Christian mystics, the Sufis, Haiku masters of Zen Buddhism, wandering poet-saints of Medieval India, forest songs of indigenous people.

The second section, "Jesus Loves Wine," contains poems for the Mystical Marriage.

The language of mystical love spans East and West, uniting the great world religions. We find its universal symbols on the lips of Yogi and Troubadour, Sufi and Cistercian monk.

Yes, we find this language of love in the Biblical Song of Songs and the parables of Jesus, the poems of Hafiz and Rumi, the ecstasies of Indian saints like Mirabai, Laladev, Jnanadev and Kabir, the devotions of St. Theresa and John of the Cross.

We may sing of Christ and the Magdalene, Shiva and Shakti, Radha and Krishna, Allah and the breath of Ruh; we may sing of Father Sky and Mother Earth; we may sing of the bee in the rose: but it is all one marriage hymn, about the bridal chamber in our own heart, the wedding of Spirit and Flesh in our own sacred humanity.

After reading these poems, one might inquire, what is my spiritual practice? I walk barefoot in wet grass at midnight, un-naming the stars.

Fred LaMotte, August 31, 2013

WOUNDED BUD

I. THE SILENCE BETWEEN THOUGHTS

WOUNDED BUD

A wounded bud never heals, it bursts open.
This is why we need another language
for what happens to the heart.

We've been murmuring like seeds,
calling from yolks and cocoons,
incubating irresolute shadows.

But lilies roar from sap, and before they're born
all beautiful creatures drink the same fire.
Intoxicated with a new name,

let your ten thousand closed flames
burst into a world.
Get bewildered with the fragrance

of your body's grace.
In your blood are enormous suns.
Call the wounded bud a rose.

BOW DOWN

This is how God becomes dust.
Touch your forehead to the earth,

bow down to the light in your body.
When the light within lifts up your head

crying, "Do not worship me, for I am you,"
bow down, bow down.

All around you, dripping with quietness,
flowers are doing this to rain.

The golden moth that lives one day
does this to a flame, the moon

to the sun. One breath
does it to another.

Receive yourself.
Bow down and drink.

Be the mother of your heart.
This is how dust becomes God.

REMAINS

Of your mother and father, all that remains
is you.

Of the bee and flower,
just honey.

Of the master and disciple only
a quivering white braid

that pours from cup to bowl.
Why ask if there are one or two?

Compare us, my beauty, to melting snow
and give up perfection.

Take up laughter and tears.
Drown in what you are.

ELEMENT

Don't you understand what is happening tonight?
Your breath is being changed into fire.

Your blood is turning to moonlight.
Soil becomes flesh, flesh becomes air.

All is suspended in the element
which alchemists have not discovered:

Silence.

SHATTER

God meant to drop this mirror,
shattering into countless images
his perfect gaze.

That is why we meet in brokenness,
fitting our pieces together again
through each others' eyes,

until we recognize one face
with eight billion reasons
for astonishment.

DIDN'T YOU CAUSE THE SUN

Didn't you cause the sun to shine
when you opened your eyes this morning?

Didn't you make the poppy unfurl
When you left the path to walk in the golden wheat?

You did, of course you did!
And didn't your wayfaring silence discover

in the last hour of night
the thrush's song a moment before it sang?

Stop naming it madness, call it love.
Stop insisting that the head belongs to God

while passion is your private weakness.
Don't you see how this confusion causes pain?

God invented the heart, you invented the mind.
Now, between your crown and chest

are legions of angels ascending and descending
on the stairway of one silver breath.

CRUSH EVERY GRAPE

Don't take your "I" for granted.
It's the last grape to be crushed,

but the sweetest by far!
Through this final ripening

the wine knows its own flavor
and attains distinction.

STUMBLE

Blessed are you when you stumble
into your perfect dance.
Blessed are you when you trip

and fall into your planting.
God does not apologize for her mistakes.
The footprint of the lost becomes a path

and the apple tree offers her first fruit to worms.
Of a thousand scattered seeds, only one grows.
Ruthlessly forgive yourself.

Chance every moment.
This rambunctious thistle was a milkweed thread
spinning in the breath of the unknown.

Sprawl into blossom, tumble back to seed.
Curled in frozen darkness, ferment
all Winter in your white hot potency

until she wakens you whispering,
"Whirl again, little one,
there are no mistakes!"

HER BOW

Without her my mind
is an arrow without a bow.
I only point and wait.

She bends into emptiness,
the moon-swollen void.

I lie across her womb,
a radius of desire.

To fire me, she lets go:
already the target trembles
with the infinitesimal tip

of the long arched journey
that was always inside her,

one circle breathed
into the center of another.

Men think they act, hunt, win,
but a Mother's secret bending
decides everything.

ANAHATA

There's a heart within your heart.
When this one beats
that one sings about light,

the gong in the atom's hollow,
photons echoing a golden bell
never struck.

This sound could only mean one thing:
a Lover whispering your name
before you were conceived.

Why should your flesh be filled with
anything but music?

YOUR BEAUTY (A PROSE POEM)

It's not enough for me to tell you that you have a beautiful soul. You are beauty. Every atom of your flesh is a universe on fire.

Your breath, your secret smile in sleep, your hip's tilt and ambled sway, the tingle of wet grass on your bare feet, your

wrinkles and soft spots, the skip of your mortal heart, your moments of silence and shadow, the mistakes you make and things

you leave unfinished, settling just where eternity intended them. I think birds sing not to wake you, but because you are awake…

You are the pure original nakedness at whom stars tremble. I love your sacrament of bathing, eating dessert, the landscape of your body rising and falling under the close and distant moon:

beauty that can't be helped!

ENTROPY CONTAINS A COUNTER-FORCE

Dancers risk whirling beyond their bodies.
Who can say how many months it takes
the moon to travel the width of a seed?

The stars are in free-fall, yet repose
in their appointed places.
Entropy contains a secret counter-force

that orders complexity into a rose,
circling whatever needs to be circled.
Therefor expand your embrace.

Hug more of the impossible.
Stumble from center to center and call it
prayer... Beyond your arms,

almost out-distanced now
by widening silence, the voice
of your Creator shouts the last law:

"Keep doing what you love!"

REAL GARDENS

There is a sky-blue rose, its petals
softer than the air it blossoms in,

springing neither from earth nor heaven,
but from the darkness inside, where real gardens grow.

It winds about the trellis of this body,
I am tangled in its fragrance.

When I'm thirsty like a bee,
I can suck the nectar of love from it.

There's enough for everyone,
and if you'd like such flowers to grow in you,

speak to me in silence:
I know where the seeds are.

WHO BEATS MY HEART? (A PROSE POEM)

I can't keep track of my atoms. I don't even know the number of cells in my fingertip. I have no idea how to command my molecules, "Rearrange yourselves for I have just drunk wine!"

At night when I'm sleeping, who breathes me? Who beats my heart, and how much do I owe him?

When I meditate, who orders my battery of neurons to synchronous firing? Who whispers, "chill out" to my adrenal gland?

And when I wake in the morning, who shouts to my pituitary, "Less water, more fire!"

I asked a scientist to explain all this, but he couldn't measure the light-years in a single atom. I asked a guru, but he just mumbled in some lost language full of M's.

How do you expect me to balance my checkbook? I can't even count my electrons, or tell you who performs this body of miracles?

SPACE FOR RENT

In heaven there's a sign:
"This Space for Rent."
God lives down here now.

He loves to walk barefoot on our dusty roads
brushing the cheek of the child
who trots along beside him.

He reaches out to hold the contagious hand.
He pauses to fill the mad woman's eyes with his.
Their faces are mirrors leaning together,

hollow corridors of wonder…
We're all like that, just lead and emptiness
polished by his glance.

He came here for this gazing.
What sparkled in the stars shines
inside us now. Think I'm kidding?

Try this breath.

A WORLD WITHOUT METAPHOR

We do not say, annihilate the ego.
We do not say, expand the mind.

Why cease to be? Or why enlarge
the cause of our sorrow?

We simply say, suffer the unutterable
ecstatic explosion of Now.

See who survives this ruinous beauty
where all that vanishes with time

is who we never were.
The world is not a metaphor.

That is why in warm leaf-lifting wind
the temperature of our breath,

three red-tailed hawks against a gray cloud
swollen with Spring rain

circle a meadow near Unionville, Pennsylvania
where a tall chestnut fille

bows her black mane, drifting through buttercups,
munching her path

like nothing in all the world
but herself.

WHIRL

Don't just shine, be darkness.
Don't polish your cup, become wine.

Take those old commandment bones
and stuff them with ambiguous sweet marrow.

Ponder withered creeds, soak them
in the nectar of uncertainty.

Make soup out of holy things
and you will sleep soundly again.

Be God's backbone, shaped like a question mark,
a massive little ovum packed with promiscuous seeds.

Be the dragon of impatience in the egg,
biting your tail and dancing upside down.

A closed box of echoes now, the scripture
once was a lyre in the breeze.

Shahadah, "No God but God!"
was a map for wandering voices,

leading songs home to silence, focusing the yolk,
an eye in the albumin typhoon.

The umbilical oar is broken now,
the goal belongs to the pathless.

You might have remembered the end of your journey
before you even started

had you not fasted from the sweetness
of what was never forbidden.

MAJNOON'S STORY

I fell in love with Layla, the king's daughter, but she was betrothed to the Prince of Light.

I did not yet know that she was my soul, cast up out of sea-foam, already lying unveiled in the shell of my heart.

So I became a wanderer, and went mad in the forest. Every bursting bud was her mouth. Every bee, stinging the wildflower, drank from my kiss.

I spun seasons with my yearning, turned Winter to Spring with my desire; bled under a pine, praying to meet her in death.

Now listen, friend, when you thirst enough for the Gift of her face, you will comprehend a way of inebriation that imbibes nothing but the nectar of moonlight: a way to make love with the eternal Virgin.

I call this way "bewilderment," because it takes place in the forest, through the wildest most pathless discipline: but you may call it a gushing wound.

Yes, it opens my chest, a fountain of darkness, effusing a great final sigh, signifying that I have surrendered to the purity of No Restraint.

You're not understanding this? I don't care! The gash in my heart encompasses both ignorance and perfect knowledge; it sucks in the universe, and the uncreated space beyond.

Like a swollen berry on a withered vine, I drop from my body.

Pan's feet press me through the sieve of the earth, into a barrel made of oak and rosewood, and other trees from the center of the Garden.

"You aren't juice any more!" says my crusher. "That was for children and pretenders. I turn you into wine, so that those who get drunk on your songs will remember everything."

This is my story, lovers and friends. This is how a drop of sorrow can sweeten the whole cup!

SPARROW'S HEART

Wake in the whisperless prayer of listening.
Repose in yesterday's wounds:
that which is bruised must still be alive.

Now ease out of pain into something more fragrant,
Presence itself, a swollen lily
unfolding its golden dust.

The God in the sparrow's heart will feed you.
The smallest of feathered things sings your song:
"I Love, therefor I Am."

DROPPED

The Beloved is known for loose behavior,
laughing, sighing, dropping things.

You fall from his open palm, he picks you up;
and if you have wounds and bruises,

he'll play music through them. You exist
through the craft of God's exquisite mistakes.

O Wounded One, with your hollow places,
don't you want to become his flute?

LIVING SILENCE

A Living Silence will be here
whether I breathe or disappear.
Whether I swoon, or die, or sleep,

some Autumn butterfly will kiss
this dewy petal in a golden haze,
and living Silence surely keep

you whole for all your nights and days.
Prism the stars in a falling tear,
my presence in your formless bliss.

MATINS

The way Mary's heart contains him, a grail;
the way stars fall through the void, in stillness;

the way a wound heals by remaining open;
the way "flight" may mean longing or grace.

The way we drink love to the dregs, then see
ourselves reflected in that emptiness;

morning prayer.

MEN

Men who support women.
Men who care for women in pain.
Men who listen to women even when

they repeat themselves.
Men who say yes to women.
Men who praise women when their bodies become old.

Men who embrace women on earth
and not women in cyberspace.
Men who linger by forest ponds

and gaze into still water
speaking to the great Mother.
Men who travel deep into the wilderness

not to hunt and kill, not to climb the highest peak,
but just to be there.
Men who know valleys, observing the etiquette

of cedar and willow.
Men who understand that the fire in their belly
is the Goddess.

INVINCIBLE

I don't want to be invincible.
I want to be astonished by loss.
I want to be stunned

and defeated by wonder,
shocked into a new creation
where only dancing is allowed.

I want to fall down again and again.
How close can my head come to your toes
before it shatters into spirals of gold?

Lift me up, I'll do
what a fountain does to sunbeams.
Step on me, I'll be the sky.

HONEY THIEF

Honey thief, marauder, slip in and out of the lily.
Steal the pollen, leave stickiness to stamen and pistil.
Press stifled cries of beauty out of the ordinary.

Filch yourself from the unselved, ravel up
silver filaments of possibility.
Spacious as the light-year in a photon,

luster the Earth with a blink
of your instantaneous night.
Antenna scented, little feet dripping

borrowed sweetness, sober in the crush
of vintner's art and bee's craft, come, distil
the nectar of the very berry from which you refrain.

O seducer of poems from the things they are about,
yes you, Transparency, do not forget:
you are the imageless and empty lens, flute hollow

before the music gushes through it, tunnel between
stars, where nothing remains but light untangling
itself from what is not there.

BURST

Some random ray from a distant sun
touches the bundled blossom of your heart
and the whole garden explodes:

jasmine, poppy, chrysanthemum,
Jesus, Krishna, Muhammad,
all mingled in a single fragrance;

nameless wildflowers too,
you and I among them.
We're planted inside

each other,
seeds just waiting
to burst.

FAITHFUL

I fall in love 12,000 times a day
like the bee in a garden,

promiscuous with all the flowers,
yet faithful

to honey.
Kiss everything, friend,

but only for an instant:
be married to One alone.

DIFFERENCE

Take the wild rose in your hand.
Here is your mistake.

You assume that God is the cause.
But God is just as bewildered as a rose.

The difference? God doesn't search
for an answer, just rides astonished waves,

spirals ever outward and inward
on petals of fire, like yours.

The difference?
You have yet to fall into what you see,

but God has dissolved
into leaves, veins, and every diaphanous wing.

FANA'

In Sufism, Fana' is the final stage, annihilation of self in God.

I dipped a cupful from your sky,
it was no longer blue.

That's what happens when the I
is taken out of you.

Hide yourself in less and less,
but I will still be there,

the sapphire in your emptiness,
the azure in your air.

RIPPLES

Be thrown, be abysmal,
be widening ripples after the pebble disappears.

Ring me in vanishing circles and let me
surround you.

We're waves of one another now.
Love's generous center only knows

how to open, how to widen what is hollow,
how to tremble with another's stillness.

Of course, I am speaking of tier upon tier
of petals in a white chrysanthemum;
and the way worlds float up in a pool of hidden grace,
like water lilies.

Earth is the one
that just blossomed.

A SECRET

Now that it's midnight
and the noise has stopped,
I'll tell you a secret.
You are the candle.
God is the moth.

CELEBRATE YOU

Listen! Chickadees, stars and unborn children
all sing, "thank you, so grateful you are here!"

spilling from your eyes, glistening from the tips
of you bones, the liquor of your spine

condensed and clustered in delicious selves;
the rainbow weeping, running all its colors

into one pure light around your precious body;
a nimbus of whispers, a kinesthesia of thank you's,

chords of pastel voices resolved into your flesh.
Hear what every creature wants with a kiss

to sing to you this day: "I come from your breath!"
Why not taste the causeless joy of the dance

that no one else can do? Be incomparable,
be the source of your own peculiar glory.

DIALOGUE

"I will wound you for free."
"But I want to pay for it."

"This will cost you everything."
"I have already given that."

"Then give me your silence,"
Love said.

So I renounced the mind and dove
into the space between thoughts

where I swam all night among moonbeams
with creatures who glowed in namelessness.

Just before dawn, Love severed off my crown
with a scimitar of sweetness, a wave of stillness,

mirage of emptiness, sword of the Prophet,
forever slicing One in Two, for the sake of devotion.

"Take that!" Love said.
"Thank you!" cried Bewilderment,

breaking the silence, opening
the wound again.

WHERE THE BEES HAVE GONE

The bee has returned for more,
but not here.

Once there was honey in this world,
but not now.

God only drinks what spills.
Somewhere the heart flowers with compassion.

That is where the giver is drunk with giving,
each stranger welcome as a bride,

and there is sweetness for wanderers.
Every stem becomes a cup,

every mouth a yearning,
every pilgrim finds the heart of the poppy.

Our world could be like this again
if we remembered how to spill.

PLANTING

Try not to rise above your longing.
Sink deeper, plant pain in the earth.

Try not to rise above your weariness.
Sink deeper, plant sorrow in the loam.

Try not to rise above your body.
Sink deeper, plant every breath.

To the Mother, you are a seed.
Your body, your pain, your breath are seedlings.

Offer them, she will open you up
so gracefully, like a sprouted wound.

Darkness will nourish you with
infinitesimal starry voices

rising from the furrow where she spilt you.
Beauty is an underground power.

It knows how to ascend,
just as it knew how to fall.

What has no name meets no resistance.
Something green, ineffably innocent

trembles out of your broken heart.
Here's the secret:

the warmth that draws us upward
is inside.

WILD IRIS

To be is perfect joy.
This is why flowers are speechless.

Each petal reveals an ancient secret:
creation is not a Word.

You could be a wild iris seeded by stray wind,
bursting by a ruined fence beyond the empty barn,

where pigeons startle and flash in dusty sunbeams
stuttered through chinks of warped cedar.

Don't try to say it.
The passion in the fragrance of evening shadows

is all that matters, boding good rain.
There is a gaze through whom silence spills

from mirror to mirror its useless beauty
in streams of not pretending to know.

Be like this. At day's end,
feign no more knowledge

than when you awoke.
Trellised on that ruined fence,

bend under graces of weightless sky,
entwined with every weed of revelation.

Flower without trying
and be wild.

CONTRADICT THYSELF

Scholars in Egypt recently discovered a transcription of the original stone tablet given to Moses on Mt. Sinai. The tablet contained the first commandment: "Contradict Thyself." But since humans were not ready for this, Moses shattered the stone. Here is the complete transcription:

Contradict Thyself.
Be foolish and wise, joyful and sad,

immaculate and sensuous.
Be radiant blackness, empty and full.

Less than an atom, encompass galaxies.
Be the fallen Virgin and the youthful Crone.

Be the Mother and the Son.
Rebel, surrender, have faith and believe in nothing.

Be still in the fury of the dance, find power in helplessness,
gentle as a warrior, wrathful as a dove defending her nest.

Enlighten your heart through un-knowing.
Discover wisdom through laughter.

Make work your play.
Remember that the opposite is also true: this stops the mind.

Let God be a pebble, let a pebble be God:
this is why you have a body.

Celebrate dying, be unborn.
Gaze into this violet and become the sky.

LIAR

I asked the flower to forgive me for not staying,
"But I have another appointment."
There too, after one drink, I regretted,

"Thank you, but no thank you."
All day long, I declined,
but I was a thief and a liar.

Now my wings are drenched with wine.
Join me in the honeycomb!
We'll feast all night in the garden of the heart.

WORK

There is a secret work inside our work,
the vocation of Presence,

the stillness at the heart
of every moment.

The energy for this labor comes from gratitude,
the connection a petal has with the sun.

Melt and stir the butter of doing
into Being.

See how a white-throated sparrow
is busy with its song.

WORLD'S END

Yesterday you were the Second Coming.
Today at sunrise, the Last Judgment began.

The Original Sin was to cover your nakedness
and flee from the Garden of this moment.

All that burns in hell is your illusion
that anything was ever wrong.

Scattered petals are the consequence of having passed
through an apocalypse of sweetness.

What happens between the sun and the rose
is consensual.

Love is the end of the world.

WASHING

Wash the dust from your smile with tears.
Trying to be happy has made you stiff.

Frown boldly, fall down, unpolish yourself.
Cleanse your forehead with grass and soil.

Into your bright wound rub the tincture
of darkness: God is all of you.

KISS

Drink the full moon
into the night between your nipples.

Hold her like breath.
Now set her back gently in the sky.

Gaze awhile and you will see
the bruise of your kisses.

She loved that. It awakened her.
That is the how God kisses the earth.

TO MY DAUGHTER (A PROSE POEM)

You enter the world like the soft pollen-fall of petals released from a mothering flower. You smile, and death becomes shy.

From one wounded wing to another I say, don't try to fly. O my beautiful daughter, best emerald of my longing, dance in eternity tonight.

Depend on the wind's breath. You are never one moment old.

TEARS OF THE BUDDHA

I have brought you thus far
teaching you to sweep away the past
with a single breath.

Now go forth with nothing
but your gentle smile, the curve
of this moment, horizon of emptiness.

A tear knows how to well up
and when to fall
even if no one is weeping.

Unless, perhaps, it is the moon
bent toward the blossoming plum.
Nothing evokes such drops of love

like being nobody!
This is how your tears become
tears of the Buddha.

YOU CHOSE ME

Does a flower choose light,
Or even know a Way
to open?

You chose me, I was closed.
But somehow the softness
of the purple aster

un-crinkled from this heart.
What petals can I offer
that are not already yours?

Such cool fire has no name.
It is the fifth season.
I call it Grace.

What can still water do
to moonbeams?
I will always wonder

why you glanced here
and shattered
this bud.

BLESSED BE THE SMALL (A PROSE POEM)

Blessed be the small. Bow down to the particular. Namaste to the missed detail that might have altered the plan.

Praise the radiant singularity of a whisker on the leathery cheek of the man who waits in line for soup and shelter.

God is even smaller than an atom. The black hole in the proton of a fern contains the information of galaxies. The hollow space between electrons hallows the infinitesimal. *Ano raniyan, mahato mahiyan.*

Let your whirlwind of seeing spiral deeper into littleness, *vippasana*, the gesture of an eye, polishing the sacred chaos of edges with perception, a sunbeam surrendering its morning Mass of photons to a petal of unfolding iris.

Satori of the finite, freedom of the bound, delectable glory of the appointed sip of tea, dissolving mind with razor grace in fractal amazement at the calculus of limits in the dot on a lady bug.

Ayn sof at the tip of lily stamen, dandylion *tattagatta*, *quidditas* of crimson-speckled moth-wing.

Whatness of the merest object bathed in wonder, a pixel of sunrise reflected in the eye of a finch, singing her ineluctable one note, *Now!*

LANDSCAPE AS LOVER (A PROSE POEM)

This land of wild forgotten gardens gone to seed, your nudity. Wheaten undulations, mountains rilled by rivers of time to muted mounds, your body now.

Disciplines of ancient yearning honed you down to this salt sweet chiaroscuro. If I were a poet I would amber you in words.

If I were a singer I would turn you on a rhythmic lathe to rhyme. If I were an artist I would layer you outrageously in tints of amaranth and fuchsia, capturing your evening glow over the sea.

If I were a virtuoso I would lean the brown swollen cello of you, balanced on one foot against my body, for a kiss of resonant emptiness, striking your tautest string like that, plucking the lower darker tone like this...

But I am a lover.

LEARN

To lift one heart uplifts the world:
this is the law within the law.
Therefor learn from the warbler at dawn,
from a pine in the evening breeze,

learn from the clear blue sky,
in whose emptiness the heart

of God dissolves,
how to bow and sing for no reason.

LAYAM

"Layam vraja: dissolve now!" ~Ashtavakra Gita

Forget the base of your spine,
the crown of your head.

Forget high and low.
Just use the wings of your heart to fall

upward into a sunlit abyss.
Don't even leap, there is no cliff.

Don't start or arrive, there is no path,
only a footloose dissolving fire.

Don't hesitate, don't look back.
Disappear without a trace

into the inconceivable vastness
of the next moment.

Why step gingerly from wick to wick
searching for a better candle?

Just stay right here
and burn.

MEETING BUDDHA ON THE ROAD

I met the Buddha on the road
and tried to kill him...

But he used some Ninja stuff
and beat me. He took my wallet,

not the money, just threw out
all my photo ID.

Then he helped me up, put his
arm around me and we stumbled

to a working class bar
where we sat all night in the back room

sipping Wild Turkey,
laughing about our minds:

how they invented suffering,
how they invented happiness,

how they invented "good" and "evil"
and their need for education,

how they invented "God" and finally
"authority," then gave it away

to some empty suit they never
even met in Washington DC,

how they invented War,
My God, how they invented War...

Gray dawn, rainy day, no flower.
Buddha slipped away.

I wondered if I hadn't just been
talking to myself all night.

GARDEN'S END

True lovers abandon this word, "love."
It is no substitute for a thud of plums
dropping in the mist at dawn,

cocoons where leaves were,
invisible pulse in furrows of sky
as dauntless ganders beat Southwest,

berries swelling with moonlight, loon
mourning, pine breeze, fallowed sweetness
of the naked Winter garden, grace

of whole afternoons without speech,
nothing but the silence
of what things are.

AUTUMN AFTERNOON (A PROSE POEM)

I don't understand a thing.

I don't understand this monarch butterfly in a golden sunbeam on the withering clematis.

I don't understand why siren hummingbirds snicker over their abundance, such sap, such ointment streams!

I don't understand why this makes me laugh with joy, or how a little sliver of moon still flutters in the blue sky.

I don't understand a single woman or the red glow of wine. I don't understand where this breath came from, or what I did to deserve it.

I don't understand why there is just enough of everything, or why this moment is so vast and overflowing with silence.

I am blessed. I am lucky to be bewildered. I am insanely proud of myself for just being here!

A BEE TREE

This Sunday morning, go to another church:
a golden-chain Laburnum in your own back yard.

Under spilling butter blossoms hear the Om
of seven hundred honey bees,
low hum in the Mother's green belly,

blue chanting tone of sky, trembling mantra
through the leaves and twigs of your body.

Lift your arms and listen, close your eyes,
surrender to the golden drone...
Don't let them tell you bees are gone.

Don't let them tell you trees are gone,
or that Paradise is elsewhere.

GENEROSITY

We're in this forgetting together, friend.
My silence is yours.

Someone who fell in love with you
long before you were born

now calls your name.
Don't you think I've heard that sound too?

Just saying "here am I" is not enough.
We must be very quiet.

Those who are truly generous
share their bewilderment.

TRINITY

In the beginning
the Father gazed

into the mirror of the Spirit
and saw Christ.

That mirror was the womb
of eternal silence,

for even God is mothered
by a mystery.

Then Christ gazed in the mirror
and saw You.

You too were born
of that joy!

WILLOW MOTHER AT HER GRAVE

I am thinking of the willow we rooted last May
with your ashes in an offering to the sky.

From far away I long to be with you, kneeling
again by the pond in the dew-laced alfalfa,

my hands folding your dust with your husband's,
my father's dust, into black loam

while the chestnut filly nods and swishes her tail.
It is good to die in the land where we were born.

Our hearts can rest in a light before light,
in a darkness that gives womb to darkness.

Now I almost hear the breeze whispering there
in the long green lovely willow, Mother.

VISIT

The Goddess whispered to my heart,
you are not here to suffer.

Learn from the bee.
You are here to make honey.

Visit dark sticky places
in everything that blossoms.

FINISH DROWNING

"Love bears me away where there's no longer any shore."
~Al-Hallaj

A lover cries for help, but not with words.
Prayer is that inner music, but it does not always sing
God's name.

The hollow of the spine cannot hide love's secret,
just as night cannot contain the ocean of stars.

What gushes out is a language of sighs and glances,
sometimes through the heart, sometimes through
another wound....

Haven't you felt breath hovering over your crown,
longing to anoint the soft spot?

Meditation is a churning silence
known only to rafts who let waves
have their way.

We can't tell whose reflection is shattered and tossed
across the waters of abysmal delight.

Even the moon is a simile for some other brilliance.
Friend, if you're still crying, "help!"
you haven't finished drowning.

WHEN YOUR NAME FELL

When your Name fell into my heart
every question in my mind
was answered by one breath: So'Ham.

The distance wasn't great
from crown to breastbone.
Why did the journey take 10,000 lives?

All I know is, there's a kingdom
in my chest now, whose government
is the silence of an endless glow,

whose boundaries keep circling
all others like a conch-full
of wings and sunsets.

When I stand at the center
of this radiance, I have no enemies.
Everyone I meet

is called the Friend.
The wine stain of your lips, O Lord,
is on each forehead, you keep giving

your royal power away.
Perfect strangers shout to one another,
"Come, wanderer, I'll be your home.

You live in me now.
The bread is light, the wine is love,
the banquet is here!"

WHAT TO DO WITH NOUNS

Richly the language of liquid nouns
rings us into flight, burning verb-wise.
You lotus my blood and hummingbird me.

Elk my sinews and cougar my skin.
Heart my hope and earth me, fur.
I garden your kisses and loam your toes.

Chrysanthemum my hand,
I will diamond your tomorrow,
just as I eternitied your yesterday.

God me, mountain my atoms,
heaven the hollow of my bones,
dis-eye my light for clearer seeing.

Now un-Word me, dance.
Galaxy my midnight with new selves.
We'll pebble and jungle, planet and sun.

I'll angel your body,
and together
we will animal the sky.

THE NAME OF THE WOUND

What the bud calls a wound
we call blossoming.

This is how the angels see
our gashed and broken places.

They keep singing, "Stay open, stay open!"
Don't you know that through your tears

that world flows as light
into this one?

II. JESUS LOVES WINE

WANDERERS WELCOME

"We seldom notice how each day is a holy place where the Eucharist of the ordinary happens." ~John O'Donahue

Out beyond Christianity
Mary Magdalene and Jesus are dancing
in a garden where things grow wild,

where things grow simply into what they are.
Many paths lead here, not one,
and the gates are always open.

Over each there is a sign that says,
"Wanderers Welcome."
Mary thinks Jesus is less like a god

than a gardener, and he is.
They drink the wine that turns
these temples into bodies again.

She reaches out to take his hand,
and he lets her.
There are three rules here:

Yearn, Risk Everything, Connect.

DON'T SEND JESUS DOWN

Don't send Jesus down to the wine cellar,
he's not your butler!
Go down yourself, drink silence, savor the dark.

When all the guests have departed except
that special someone,
take out your best bottle, one drop of which

is sweeter than the night you were conceived.
Now there was a night: but it won't be the last!
Each grape from this vineyard is a night like that,

bursting with starry blackness.
The wine seems clear and tasteless,
but a single sip is stronger than death.

Top off your special someone's cup
with the sound of spilling diamonds
again and again until you're both

one dance, one void-stained kiss!
At sunrise, maybe you'll learn
your lover's name.

ISHQ

Because your sighs have fermented my blood,
I need no wine.
My name on your lips is the longest Sura.

I begin the Night Journey in your eyes,
toward a wild desert fragrance.
The only revelation is my face reflected in your gaze.

Keep your window open: do not turn
this emptiness to glass, lest you profane
the Prophet's word, and make seeing an eye.

Without the savor of your presence, coupled with a kiss,
my senses are stone, the very thought of love an idol.
Ignore the image engraved inside your skull:

like a lover's map, it was sketched by trembling.
Look instead to hollow seeds before conception,
where zero became one in the bright space of unknowing.

We are each other's search for what's between mirrors,
this wilderness of purity: you, the last veil of my desire,
and I, the veil within that, translucent,

blue, the color of yearning sky.
Spin quickly now before the other vanishes,
so that we may catch God at the center of whirling.

You lit me on the wick of your eye
where I danced as seeing.
From the golden oil in my bones, I kindled you,

a soul for my soul, gushing through my wounds.
Anoint me! Drip down this broken necklace
of seven dangling pearls.

From throat to thigh, unite the sea and setting sun.
Of purple curtains in the King's chamber we may speak,
but never of what happens on the other side!

When dawn comes, we'll whisper
which of us was stillness,
which the dancer.

THE TAVERN IN MY HEART

At the tavern in my heart there's a name on the door
that turns all other words to laughter,
but I can't pronounce it when I get this way.

I just dance in the street and shout at people
who pretend to ignore me.
But now and then when I'm sober, I start howling:

Don't go to work today, don't pay off those debts!
Your sins are too vast! Just step in here
and taste some bewilderment.

The inn keeper won't bill you till the end of time.
Then you can tell him, "It's all your fault,
your hospitality made me tipsy!"

Friend, this wine is better than breast milk.
When nothing's left, you'll see
the Beloved's face gazing

from the bottom of your cup.
Then you'll sing like me:
"This is the emptiness we all adore!"

WHIRLED APART

The wind that whirls us apart is not cruel.
It too is the breath of the flute.

Lips of the shepherd calling the scattered
can't press the hollow reed all night:

He breathes in, we fall into a silence
between the notes: this too is music.

Let it open some distant flower
in another garden.

I keep echoing inside you, and even your
forgetting is filled with me.

Bear witness: you will hear a faint breeze.
Love makes us strangers for the sake of prayer.

IMBOLC (THE FEAST OF ST. BRIGID)

When this season arrives, a dark forgotten well
starts gushing again, the creek bed in my spine,

marrowed with moss and babbled with pebble song,
more local to the bone than basil or thyme.

Lower than roots, my juice still in its breathless stone,
I fall for a wanderer with uncombed maidenhair,

a shepherdess reclining on her elbow,
dangling fern fingers, sapling hips of pine

splayed from a nurse log. Slow as evening,
gestures of mushroom and cedar frond conceal

last summer's light. Her feet are rain on huddled wolves.
She's thistle in the apple's roots, a plum twig

twisted in her dream of seeds, secret fragrance
I'd fast and starve these thirsty lips all winter for,

groping for the milk of her name. Now friend,
abandon words and wander into the ground.

LADY BREATH

One breath takes the hand of another and leads her
up into the balcony, where we gaze at falling stars.

One breath takes the hand of another and leads her
down the spiral staircase, past the rose garden of the heart,

to the cellar of blushes where dark fruit, dangled
at the tip of exhalation, drops, suddenly fermented

by a hushed and ancient shadow (it's an endless moment).
No longer two, breathing whispers a sweet secret

to its own stillness, thus conceiving galaxies down
in root musk where eternity tangles around the sacrum,

gnarled crone-tendrils from whose moon-drenched
Shakti swollen pearls emerge in milk foam,

nascent virginal effluvium of worlds glistening over
the body of Her who is suddenly never not just born,

the star-sighed maiden, dallying through this
honeymoon in the mansion of my chest, pregnant

now with all the spheres by which I am contained:
sweet Lady breath, take my hand.

BANQUET

We don't create this world of laughter and weeping.
It's poured into our cup at the wedding.
We're not the center of creation:

we're the tilt and wobble that makes
the spinning finally come to rest.
No heart beats itself: something else

whips us like cream into this sweetness
and dollops a little of us onto everything.
Don't be a guest, be the feast.

The host will fill your cup again and again.
He'll whisper your name and remind you
of that summer night you couldn't tell the difference

between moonbeams, fingers, bees and pollen.
You were planted then: you burst open now.
The sign of recognition is falling inward

from a great height, and never reaching
the bottom of the grail.

LADY OF THE SKY

We all want to see the smile of our first parents
when they fell in love.

The sun is waiting, she will not breathe out
 until she sees That on your face!

Then she will become your partner,
the Lady of the Sky.

You have a certain work to offer her,
the work of your joy.

No one but you can do it.
That is how you support her.

Where else would the Lady find light?
Discover your task, do only That.

Speak only That, love only That.
You will never weary of saying

Thank You, and the Lady of the Sky
will bear you children, countless seeds

in every blossom, countless flowers
in every seed, ten thousand gold

and blue petals from one hollow root.
Surely the stem of your smile

undulates through still green waters
in muddy secret forest pools,

the lotus ponds of your flesh.
This kind of radiance comes from the belly.

Where one breath pours into another,
offer all your darkness.

MAMBO LINE

This mambo line we've been dancing in all night:
I've forgotten where it started, your place or mine?

And who are all these whirling fools,
their hands on one another's buttocks?

Preening, prancing, behaving like Democrats,
pointing their tail feathers up at the sun?

Oh I admit, I'm one of them,
bragging about my torrid love affair with God;

drinking too much and shouting,
"We weren't invited to this! We just showed up!"

O Jesus, you were a homeless poet once,
eating leftovers from the lawn parties of the upright.

You know what it means to scavenge among the wasted seeds,
looking for the sprouted ones, the ones with laughter inside.

We're like jostling crows on a live electric wire,
inebriated with the voltage: everyone's looking for juice!

If one of us touched the ground, we'd all be dead.
But that won't happen, we're never coming down!

We only move in one direction now, like black flames.
I'm so dizzy and mad with midnight dancing,

whirling out of your embrace, falling back into your heart,
I can't tell which of us I am!

I think I may be sober now in the stillness before dawn:
I can almost remember your name.

If I do, I won't tell the others: I just want to know,
last night, was I the wine or the cup?

ONLY ONE WORD

There is only one word. It begins
in the awe at the back of your throat
and ends in breathless pressed lips, closed eyes,

a single syllable containing every alphabet
and every language from infancy till death:
the lover's sigh, precarious laughter on a cliff,

the stunned gargle of soldier's blood.
All other sounds are echoes, reverberations
in empty canyons of memory and hope.

If you would be a poet, keep trying
to pronounce it, even if it kills you.
Be like a thief fleeing from a royal garden,

attempting to breathe through a mouth
stuffed with stolen figs.
Even if the King runs after you, shouting,

"Wait, you're welcome here, our fruit is yours!"
keep fleeing into wild places
until you find the well of silence.

What sound is your breath making now?
Look in the blossoming weeds, each tiny
petal scribbled with a syllable of prayer!

Pause, part your lips.
Now drink....
This is the Beloved's name.

ABANDON

With every breath, I abandon my vow
to refrain from astonishment.

Calling your name unravels my most
carefully woven robes, I spill

into the space between the planets and the sun.
I cannot resist undressing my formlessness.

Transparency becomes you, love.
Churned to honey, your darkness drips down

from the stem of my brain
and curls my toes with delight.

Your taste is too strong for me; even a little
makes me foolish and wise, makes me pour

everything into the crescent moon cup of my heart
where breathing stops, seduced, dissolved

like sugar in wine.
Offer me lemons now, yarrow and ginger.

I'll warm them in the same secret bowl
of prayer and yearning.

Our aroma turns stars tipsy; they spin, we blush,
each of us a rose in the other's cheek.

COMMANDMENT

God has commanded us to splurge
on everything beautiful:
lentil soup, pumpkins, scent of autumn rose,

sound of a mockingbird in the withered cornfield
under a full moon,
warmth of hands circled around fire,

the hidden factory of gold in a chloroplast,
leaf nectar, your mother's
honeycomb gift of flesh,

and the strong dark wine of silence...
Drink, pass the cup,
fear no abundance:

all that is lovely is yours.
God isn't interested in discipline.
Even emptiness tastes like butter

dripping over the stars.
The distance from earth to sun
smells like cooked sugar.

Eternity is the fragrance
seeping through the risen loaf
of your body.

Savor nakedness,
drop the old law, "Thou shalt not,"
in a moist furrow.

Just whisper one word
to your starved heart:
"Feast!"

CROSSROAD

At the center of your body is a crossroad
where journeys end, journeys begin.
Meet me here, I will change you like a beam

refracted through a lens of sap.
You will change me like a meson, colliding
with the darkest particle of its other self.

Scattered and gathered again,
be made of light, rest in pathlessness.
Become a wandering gust of secrets.

The circle was full before it breathed
a moon, an embryo, a soul.
Find your way home by getting lost

in every direction: this is called the center.
Wander through me as I wander
through you: this is called the heart.

Arrive, speaking the Master's word.
Depart, singing your own song.

A WEDDING

This wedding was arranged by the Elders
before the Bride and Groom were ever two.
Don't worry, they know what One becomes.

They choose the soul to marry your body.
You've been stumbling down the aisle too long,
wondering if you're ready for this.

You make eyes at the guests in their pews:
"Should I marry this fellow instead?"
Stop doubting, stop tripping over your gown.

Stop chatting with strangers and cousins.
Just gaze toward the sanctuary
at the one who awaits you there.

Pour your gladness into that face.
Graft your vine to that vineyard tonight
and priest, bride, groom, wedding

will all get crushed in the dancing.
After you say "I do,"
these grapes become wine.

PAIN

Angels long to be born on earth
to feel this pain.

Our distance is their breath,
given for us to sigh.

They only dream of this,
we sense it as a mortal chest wound.

They gaze into one waveless light,
we have sunrise and sunset

with oceans between us.
They see a storm of brilliance in blue emptiness

as they approach your beating heart.
They watch over buds and cocoons.

Where we swim in nectar, they see wings
and flowers, and they envy us, not bitterly

but with their own celestial discontent
and yearning for entanglements

that can only be unraveled on earth.
One petal unfolding in darkness here

is better than a thousand years in heaven:
therefor we love.

RADHA'S LAMENT

O Shyam, the Gods are asleep,
the garden spills moonlight from every flower.

The law and the prophets are hidden like stars,
outshined by another brightness.

It is the hour for the instrument of breath,
and the melody of yearning.

Time for sighs to play on the body's secret strings,
and toes to dance in stinging dew.

I am made hollow by the silence
that follows the whisper of your name.

Sundara, your nearness empties me.
My chest is a panting doe.

A touch of your teasing straightens my spine.
I could be lifted and played by breeze or moonbeam.

Promiscuous wind through withered vines;
buds appear.

Your singing through broken places;
breasts fill with milk.

Lovers' bodies sparkle with diamonds and pearls,
but I wear blossoms of darkness:

seven voids
of surrender...

CONCEIVE

Beloved, bewildered and wild,
you fill me with my heart.

Though pure, though one alone, you pour
your soul into my mold, a golden art,

create a cup of otherness,
two roses from one molten ore.

Now, love, conceive a mother's bliss.
Bear yourself, and fill *your* heart with child.

BRIDAL CHAMBER

"Jesus loved Mary Magdalene more than all the disciples,
and he used to kiss her often..." ~Gnostic Gospel of Philip

Between outbreath and inbreath
I hold space for you.

Come meet me here in secret, Mary.
No one will see your perfect nakedness.

No one will know how waves
of silence ravished your darkness

with kisses of light.
Ten million stars longed for this.

Your beauty was known to them before
the Maker's.

They made themselves, desperately imitating
your innocence.

APPROACH

The moon is full.
Barely audible footsteps
on forest moss…

A tiny ankle bell, a single
breath on a wooden flute?
Or only midnight

breeze among the cedars?
Silence again…
Whoever is coming

wants to be heard!
A little time for longing
to arise in Radha's heart…

AFFAIR

Confess!
You are having a secret love affair
with your Anger,

that ruby-fanged serpent,
that Autumn moon coiled in your belly.

You coax her quivering tongue
with the wand of certainty,
the prod of moral conviction,

stirring political sparks in her poison sack.
The shades are drawn in the chamber

of being right.
Come out and dance
naked in the foolishness of morning,

where love drops her veil of madness
and the sun melts creatures into ghee.

THE GARLAND

There is another kind of desire,
made from the same grapes

but aged in darker places, longer,
in barrels of oak from wood

more wild than the garden of believing.
Too strong for Jesus to serve Peter:

he saves this wine for Mary, his Nadeema,
celebrating the death of every law

but one: "Become your yearning."
This is the vintage that casts out demons

and makes souls drunk with prayer.
The garland he hangs on her shoulders

breaks with the whirl of their dance.
Enormous blossoms spill from her throat

to her belly like unloosened heavens,
their angels in free-fall, delighted

to fill her loins with unborn children
and seeds of glory.

THE MARRIAGE OF SH'HAQA AND Z'FARA

To sing the music of the heart,
there are two Arabic words:
Sh'haqa the inbreath, *Z'fara* the outbreath.

See, in the language of the holy Koran,
everything has gender: *Sh'haqa*
steals into the bridal chamber,

Z'fara the vessel for what pours,
then ferments and bubbles over.
See, even ordinary words teach us

about what cannot be spoken:
the truffles under your breastbone,
the opal and onyx of breathing.

These lovers need a place in your body
to formalize their vows of astonishment.
Who will pronounce them husband and wife

if not you? Your twin entwining selves,
they whirl in empty garments of light
until the last exhalation.

What lies beyond that final sigh
cannot be known.
All we know is this: to breathe is prayer.

TRANSMUTATION

Carry the pollen of sexual yearning
to the hive of your golden soul.

Whatever blossoms on earth
can be turned into honey.

This is how sounds become luminous
and the garden shares one fragrant light,

how cocoa beans ferment
and tongues get sweet without sugar.

This is how Gopis are in God
and bridesmaids meet the Groom,

how heaven and earth, sap and petal
are one body.

On the border of the flesh and its aura
there's a marketplace for atoms of delight.

The contraband is innocence,
the price is love.

Jesus was a bee-keeper, Mary a maker of mead.
So keep the secret, and store up radiance.

WOUNDING FOR FREE

"I will wound you for free."
"But I want to pay for it."

"This will cost you everything."
"I have already given that."

"Then give me your silence,"
Love said.

So I renounced the mind and dove
into the space between thoughts

where I swam all night among moonbeams
with creatures who glowed in namelessness.

Just before dawn, Love severed off my crown
with a scimitar of sweetness,

wave of stillness, empty mirage,
sword of the Prophet,

forever slicing One in Two
for the sake of devotion.

"Take that!" Love said.
"Thank you!" cried Bewilderment,

breaking the silence, opening
the wound again.

POUR

Pouring out jugs of sweet emptiness,
we got drunk on an overflowing void
while we were still each other.

Even today, we can't tell the difference
between darkness and light,
so we just sizzle away.

The old earth dissolves into a new one
every time we blink.
There's a roar that roses make

when they burst at midnight
cupped in the palms of the moon.
We hear it when we breathe;

some Goddess chained inside us,
caramelizing the sugar in our spines.
Remind me again, drunken partner,

what the password is for entering
the kingdom of silence.

LOVE'S FEW WORDS

Love has such
a limited vocabulary,

forgetting even
the simplest words
like right and wrong,

should and shouldn't,
best and worst,

until, unable to think at all,
love takes refuge in Silence
where even the smallest creature,

a pebble, an aphid under a leaf,
the first blue periwinkle

is a Word of God
in a thundering chorus
of revelation.

KNEEL

Why waste your life believing
that stars are above and earth below,

only to discover too late, too late,
light gushing from every part of your body

where dancing begins?
Why travel from this world to another?

All journeys are over but deepening now.
Your heartbeat is the shaman's drum.

Don't move, be moved. One treasure
is left to find, the Radiance you were

before you started the search.
Spring is an intuition crinkled in cocoons:

your laughter can do something about that.
Ferns make fists all Winter, waiting

for you to breathe a little deeper.
Now fall among bulbs in black soil

on the one world that is really yours
and touch God's Kingdom with your knees.

TIPSY

"The sun shines for you today yes." ~Molly Bloom, Ulysses

Sparrows don't wait for dawn, they just start singing.
Plum buds feel a tug of warmth deep down blind naked twigs.

Even if you can't dance, there's rhythm in your breathing.
This round earth wants to be your whirling partner.

It's already started, this trembling of seeds
in the dust of your spine.

Separateness is just the shimmering.
Keep kneeling to kale and pumpkins in your garden.

Keep kneading the moon into your loins
until the loaf of this world is risen.

Strive ever downward toward the Divine.
Your flesh's humblest photon is the palace door.

Didn't you know? Every particle pulsates with the Psalms.
Friend, this yearning for light is light.

EVEN DARKER

Words have served their purpose.
It is time for wine.
Ferment of moonlight in plum petals,

brandy of sleeping birds cradled in holly,
vintage burgundy of midnight,
even darker wine

of silence...
It is wandering time.
Walk nowhere for hours,

amazed by the pulse of duration,
the expanding moment.
Listen for the modest sigh

of starlight in the pine.
Taste the distillate sparkle
in your heart's hollow.

Come back tipsy, lover.
Do not speak of what
or whom you have known...

NEW MOON

Under a new moon, Autumn petals...
Beautiful one, our bodies perish soon.

Light itself is fickle.
Lovers should arouse each other's silence

following an eternal breath
home, to the garden of the heart.

That is where we first met,
remember?

THE SMILE

You could get organized, become
respectable, live beyond this perplexity.
But then you might wake up

one morning and discover
that your smile has escaped
like a white bird from your

careful cage, flown wild
into darkness on dewy wings,
floating over the suburbs

to look for a better mouth,
one whose lips are always
parted in a breath of bewilderment,

stained with wine and kisses.
Then some afternoon, a long time hence,
if life is more emboldened than

your dreams, you'll enter
a dim café, fleeing
from Spring showers.

You'll glance toward one of those
corner tables where
secret lovers bend, almost

touching over lukewarm cups -
and there it will be, there it will be,
On someone else's face!

TWIN-HEARTED SONNET

I need no other breast, for yours is mine.
You need no heart but this, for mine is yours,
crimsoned image in a cup of wine,
my sweeter self imbibed from second source.

Love wants reflection to be full and wise:
so we by candlelight, in pearl-soft pool
of chocolate berries and each others eyes,
taste wantonly dessert without self-rule.

Each will, if we be whole, be wholly lost
in other's cup and gaze: each holy fool
in other's heart, your face embossed

upon my inmost eye, which is both jewel
and mirror, filled with you, the final sweet
that does the supper of my love surfeit.

THIS IS NOT A LOVE POEM

"There is some kiss we want with our whole lives,
the touch of spirit on the body." ~Rumi

Don't mistake this for a love poem
about our mouths of flesh.
This is a poem about a kind of prayer

in which the darkness burns up our eyes,
our faces forget themselves in mirrors of fire,
our bodies become an exhalation of ashes

whose mingled lips are similes
for the widening touch of one Self.
Unlike plum blossoms bursting in moonlight,

our opening never closes.
In this kind of prayer I am your wick,
you are my flame.

These secrets we whisper and forget.
Knowing and unknowing, nakedness
and the wearing of wine-stained garments,

are a single kiss, obliterating faces and souls.
We are tongues tasting God,
scorching earth and sky with a song,

annihilating the notion of annihilation.
Now we rest like weary swords,
sheathed in each other's breathing.

CANCER POEM

When I discovered the lump,
you looked into my eyes and said,
"Everything will be all right."

The biopsy was positive.
But you gazed at me that way again:
"Everything will be all right."

Chemo began. I sat on my bed
wondering if I could stand up
without vomiting.

You sat down beside me.
Your eyes swam into mine
and spoke those words again.

But in six months, I was ready
to give up. You said,
"Go ahead, give up, but

Everything will be all right."
And for a year I whispered,
"I'm OK." Then I looked in a mirror

at cheeks like smoke that veils
the surface of a distant planet.
I turned away to meet those

gentler mirrors, your eyes.
The final night, I was
a paper lantern without a bulb.

On a morphine drip I couldn't
wait for the animal in my throat
to stop sucking. You came

into the room and sat down
beside me. "She can't hear you,"
they said. "Yes she can," you said.

My eyes were elsewhere but you
found them and spoke: "Everything
will be all right...." Now the mirror

has become a sea, I live in waves
of possibility swelling with light.
All day, all night, my gaze

breaks its lovely tide upon you
like this. I am always
whispering "Yes."

MAGDALENA

I was not aware that you had entered my veins.
Inebriation with your beauty is gradual
as the drift of a star through Winter nights.

Steal into these rafters, my dove, and stay.
Do not ask whether this is the flesh or the soul.
My lips, stained with your name, curve ever

so slightly, part of the infinite circumference
of prayer. You have become the delicious void
I enter as a connoisseur descends to his wine cellar.

He comes back smiling, not quite himself.
There is a dawn inside before sunrise.
It is your name. The first touch of that sound

peels the horizon back from an ocean of blue silence.
Your glance contains distance as a cup contains a vineyard,
a hundred autumns of the winemaker's discipline.

The moth of the heart teased by a candle;
are these singed wings your breaths or mine?
"Far," "further" and "away" are fluctuations of Presence.

Once before, you walked in the Garden
of Sacred Disobedience, where the Master
danced for you in veils of moonlight.

You reached out: the Gardener was not there.
Day approached with its weary sour sunlight.
Jesus, the incarnation of the ordinary,

had come and gone… Now Magdalena,
you have a second chance
to become fire instead of kindling.

Burn everything this time, throw your whole
body into love! If there are ashes,
I will smear them on my lips and eyes.

ODE TO BLUEBERRIES

Now that it's September, I want to thank blueberries.
I want to thank peaches, cantaloupes, cherry tomatoes
and corn on the cob. All summer long while we griped

about the Republicans, you were lying there in baskets,
blue eyes silently watching, blinking back tears.
Some of you were whole crimson sunsets in my hand.

I'm not sure what antioxidants are, but thank you:
I know that you were full of them.
I loved your fuzz, buxom peach, your sass, blackberry.

I loved your smile, honeydew, halved and split as we
slobbered together. Local strawberry, just one of you
gushing on my tongue was almost too much to bear!

Next summer you could do a better job of staying
under three dollars a pint; otherwise, no complaint.
How erotic you are, plum, lounging in a sunbeam,

your crimson still-life sweating in droplets of fever.
You should be ashamed how your waves imploded
on the beaches of my mouth!

Well, it was a scene. But thank you.
I also want to thank some of you flowers: begonia,
peony, chrysanthemum and lucifer crocosmia.

I do not forget the morning glory, that soft trumpet
made of sky, calling us inward toward granaries
of moonlight. And now, just as the rest of you languish,

the apples arrive! Round crimson shouts
from green caverns of Autumn afternoon.
O humans, we too might burst, an orchard of longings,

wild but rooted, globe-laden, corridored with fruit.
We too might drop at the edge of the meadow,
silvered by flurries of milkweed and thistle.

Why not bend to our ripening, the pungent smolder
of our inward sugars, the grace and gravity of our Fall?
Why not bow to the blessed sag of limbs and bruise

our knees in surrender? Lying on the bee-festered earth,
hollowed, wormed out with inward paths, and free
from every striving to rise, why not let this turning planet
have her way with us, and do what she loves?

ABOUT THE AUTHOR

Fred LaMotte is an interfaith chaplain and teacher of world religions who has served in both private secondary schools and colleges. He has taught meditation and stress management for over forty years, having studied personally with masters of India's Shankaracharya tradition. He also studied Gregorian chant and Christian mystical prayer while in residence at Trappist and Benedictine monasteries in Europe and the U.S.

Fred has degrees in literature and theology from Yale University and Princeton Theological Seminary. He lives with his wife Anna and his buddy Willy, a free-range organic golden poodle, near Seattle WA.

ACKNOWLEDGMENTS

I would like to thank Ron Starbuck of Saint Julian Press for his tireless devotion to art and spirituality; Dana Chamseddine, my inspiration and spiritual friend, a brilliant Arabic poetess who so selflessly translates my poems into Arabic; and my lovely wife, Anna, who is the incarnation of generosity.

CPSIA information can be obtained
at www.ICGtesting.com
Printed in the USA
BVOW06s0443290118
506475BV00006B/175/P